BUT WHY?

by Cassie St. Amand
illustrated by Jan Dolby

◆ FriesenPress

Suite 300 - 990 Fort St
Victoria, BC, V8V 3K2
Canada

www.friesenpress.com

ISBN
978-1-5255-8205-9 (Hardcover)
978-1-5255-8206-6 (Paperback)
978-1-5255-8207-3 (eBook)

*1. JUVENILE NONFICTION, HEALTH & DAILY LIVING,
DISEASES, ILLNESSES & INJURIES*

Distributed to the trade by The Ingram Book Company

For my sweet daughter Jackie
And all of the mothers who
made it to the sunrise - C. S.

For my forever friend Elizabeth - J. D.

I looked out the window today and the world looked so different.

Why are we home all of the time?

Because there is a virus
spreading all over the world.

What is a virus?

A virus is a teeny, tiny germ, smaller than anything you can see. A virus needs to live inside your body in order to grow and it can make you very sick.

Why do I have to move onto the grass, even with
my scooter, when people walk by?

Because the virus can spread if we get too close.
We have to practice
'social distancing.'

What is social distancing?

It means that we don't get too close to people. It means we give each other space.

Just like when I am angry
or upset and I tell you I need

- just like that.

If we keep our space from people outside of our home, we will protect ourselves and others. We will help stop the spread of the virus.

Why does the playground have yellow and red tape around it and why can't I play on it?

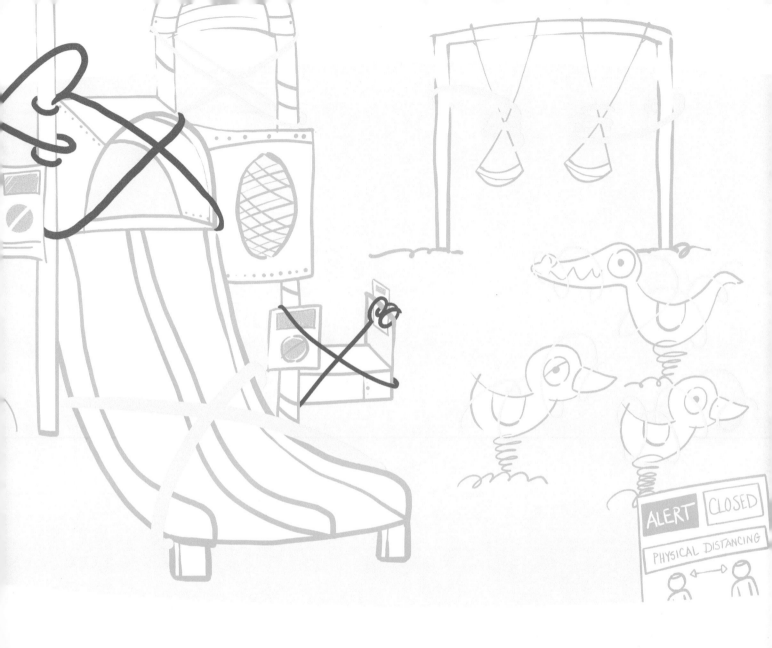

Because when you play on the playground you can get too close to others. When you touch the playground, your germs stay on the surface and others can touch them.

Why am I not going to school?
Why are you not going to work?

Because being around a lot of people means being around a lot of germs. We don't always know who has the virus. Staying away means we will help stop the spread of the virus.

Why do I need to wash my hands SO much? They really hurt!

Washing our hands means we are washing away our germs.
Washing away our germs means the germs won't get into our bodies
when we touch our face, eat our food and hug one another.

Why are the city streets so quiet?
Where are all of the people?

People are still here. Just like you and
me most are staying home. If we stay
home we aren't in large groups. When
we do this we help to stop the spread.

I see...

We all have to help.

I still don't like it.

It makes me angry
I can't play with
my friends.

It makes me
scared to
see people
in masks
everywhere.

It makes me sad I can't hug Grandma.

It makes me worried there is a virus in our world.

I DON'T like it.
I DON'T like it one bit at all!!!

I want to go to school!

I want to play
at the park!

I want to ride the bus!

Why Mom?
Why is it like this?

It is hard.
It is unfair.
I am sorry it is this way
right now.

Can I play with my
friends for just one day?

Just one?

And then I will go back to being just with our family?

I hear you.
It won't always
be this way.
It will change.

We have to keep our
distance, wash our hands
A LOT, and stay home as
much as possible.

Sigh

You will go to school again.

You will hug your grandma again,
play with your friends and swing
on the swings.

We will all do the things
we are missing again.

Our world needs to heal right now
And together that is
what we are doing.

Help to heal our world.

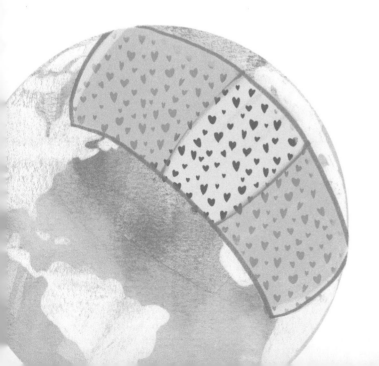

Today I look out the window and see the sunrise. I feel filled with thanks and hope knowing I am helping to heal our world.

How lucky am I?

BUT WHY?

But why do children feel so much?

Children are naturally born to express themselves in BIG ways. Children have a unique gift to be able to 'let' out emotions in a raw, true and honest form. Some scream, some become quiet, some kick and bite, and some hide or cling. The emotions show up differently and change over time. The emotions can be overt and in your face, and can be hidden.

As loving people in their lives we have the gift to support the growth of how children process their emotions. When a child (adult too) expresses BIG EMOTIONS imagine this as a FLOODED STATE. The emotions are overpowering the brain's ability to calm and flooding the pre frontal cortex, which is our area of reasoning, problem solving, and rationalization.

When these emotions show up they can be challenging and difficult to know what to do. If we truly listen to what the emotions are telling us we can help to build resilience in our children.

"Brains grow and develop as children interact with their environment. All learning is based on relationships." Dr Stuart Shaker, The Merhit Centre

So what do we do?

The key is our response to them.
Follow the ANA
(Acknowledge, Name, Accept)

ACKNOWLEDGE THE EMOTION

-Builds awareness of what is happening

-Validates what is being expressed

Use statements like:

I see... you are bothered because your lips are pushed out and your eyebrows are like this (make the face)

I hear... you are getting frustrated because your voice is getting louder and whinny

NAME THE EMOTION

See if the child can 'name' what they are feeling (angry, frustrated, worried, excited etc.)

Use statements like:

-Can you give a 'name' to what you are feeling

-If you name the feeling it will help to give it less power. It will help to make you feel better

If the child is too young or having trouble assist by using statements like:

-I see you are frustrated because you are kicking me

-I see you are angry because your face is turning red and scrunched up like this (make the face)

*Explaining what the child's physical body is doing is helpful for them to start to identify with what is happening

ACCEPT WHAT THE CHILD SAYS (even when it is hard)

-Respond with empathy and without judgment

-Be 'in' the emotion with them

-Picture jumping into the deep ocean and being in the flooded state with them

When we are in the 'flood' with them we are showing them it is 'ok' to feel these feelings and this will lower the water level and help bring them to a state of calm. For more information on how to grow resilient children go to www.cassiestamand.com

About the Author and Illustrator

As an Ontario Qualified teacher who spent her career teaching kindergarten and preschool, CASSIE ST. AMAND has read more than her fair share of children's books. A level 2 certified Self-Regulation facilitator, Cassie now owns her own preschool, Apple Jacks Preschool, and will soon be opening a new nature school, East Village School.

A parenting coach who provides guidance and support to her community, Cassie lives in Toronto, Ontario, with family.

JAN DOLBY is a children's illustrator who likes to wash her hands with lots of soap. You can see more of her work at jandolby.com.

butwhystory.com

CPSIA information can be obtained
at www.ICGtesting.com
Printed in the USA
LVHW071014011020
667542LV00002BA/68